I0867894

The Standard®

PROPELLER LOG

ASA-SP-L

THE STANDARD® PROPELLER LOG
SP-L

ASA-SP-L
ISBN 978-1-56027-418-6

Printed in the United States of America

[19] 24

Aviation Supplies & Academics, Inc.
7005 132nd Place SE
Newcastle, Washington 98059 USA
asa2fly.com | asa@asa2fly.com

TRANSPORTATION USD $7.95

ISBN 978-1-56027-418-6

50795 >

9 781560 274186

Propeller Record General Information

Propeller Manufacturer ______________________________

Model ______________________ **Type** ______________________

Hub Series # ______________________ **Blade #** ______________________

Date of Manufacture ______________________

	Make/Model	**Serial #**
Aircraft Installed On:		

☐ HUB & BLADE INSPECTIONS, REPAIRS AND ALTERATIONS

Year: ______ Date:	Total Time in Service	Description
Next Inspection Due:	Time Since Overhaul	Mech. Cert. # or Repair Station # ______

Year: ______ Date:	Total Time in Service	Description
Next Inspection Due:	Time Since Overhaul	Mech. Cert. # or Repair Station # ______

Year: ______ Date:	Total Time in Service	Description
Next Inspection Due:	Time Since Overhaul	Mech. Cert. # or Repair Station # ______

HUB & BLADE INSPECTIONS, REPAIRS AND ALTERATIONS ☐

Year: ______ Date:	Total Time in Service	**Description**
Next Inspection Due:	Time Since Overhaul	Mech. Cert. # or Repair Station # ______

Year: ______ Date:	Total Time in Service	**Description**
Next Inspection Due:	Time Since Overhaul	Mech. Cert. # or Repair Station # ______

Year: ______ Date:	Total Time in Service	**Description**
Next Inspection Due:	Time Since Overhaul	Mech. Cert. # or Repair Station # ______

☐ HUB & BLADE INSPECTIONS, REPAIRS AND ALTERATIONS

Year: _______ Date:	Total Time in Service	Description
Next Inspection Due:	Time Since Overhaul	Mech. Cert. # or Repair Station # _______

Year: _______ Date:	Total Time in Service	Description
Next Inspection Due:	Time Since Overhaul	Mech. Cert. # or Repair Station # _______

Year: _______ Date:	Total Time in Service	Description
Next Inspection Due:	Time Since Overhaul	Mech. Cert. # or Repair Station # _______

HUB & BLADE INSPECTIONS, REPAIRS AND ALTERATIONS ☐

Year: ______ **Date:**	**Total Time in Service**	**Description**
Next Inspection Due:	**Time Since Overhaul**	**Mech. Cert. # or Repair Station #** ______

Year: ______ **Date:**	**Total Time in Service**	**Description**
Next Inspection Due:	**Time Since Overhaul**	**Mech. Cert. # or Repair Station #** ______

Year: ______ **Date:**	**Total Time in Service**	**Description**
Next Inspection Due:	**Time Since Overhaul**	**Mech. Cert. # or Repair Station #** ______

☐ HUB & BLADE INSPECTIONS, REPAIRS AND ALTERATIONS

Year: ________ Date:	Total Time in Service	Description
Next Inspection Due:	Time Since Overhaul	Mech. Cert. # or Repair Station # ________

Year: ________ Date:	Total Time in Service	Description
Next Inspection Due:	Time Since Overhaul	Mech. Cert. # or Repair Station # ________

Year: ________ Date:	Total Time in Service	Description
Next Inspection Due:	Time Since Overhaul	Mech. Cert. # or Repair Station # ________

Year: ______ Date:	Total Time in Service	Description
Next Inspection Due:	Time Since Overhaul	Mech. Cert. # or Repair Station # ______

Year: ______ Date:	Total Time in Service	Description
Next Inspection Due:	Time Since Overhaul	Mech. Cert. # or Repair Station # ______

Year: ______ Date:	Total Time in Service	Description
Next Inspection Due:	Time Since Overhaul	Mech. Cert. # or Repair Station # ______

☐ HUB & BLADE INSPECTIONS, REPAIRS AND ALTERATIONS

Year: ______ Date:	Total Time in Service	**Description**
Next Inspection Due:	Time Since Overhaul	Mech. Cert. # or Repair Station # ______

Year: ______ Date:	Total Time in Service	**Description**
Next Inspection Due:	Time Since Overhaul	Mech. Cert. # or Repair Station # ______

Year: ______ Date:	Total Time in Service	**Description**
Next Inspection Due:	Time Since Overhaul	Mech. Cert. # or Repair Station # ______

HUB & BLADE INSPECTIONS, REPAIRS AND ALTERATIONS ☐

Year: ______ **Date:**	**Total Time in Service**	**Description**
Next Inspection Due:	**Time Since Overhaul**	**Mech. Cert. # or Repair Station #** ______

Year: ______ **Date:**	**Total Time in Service**	**Description**
Next Inspection Due:	**Time Since Overhaul**	**Mech. Cert. # or Repair Station #** ______

Year: ______ **Date:**	**Total Time in Service**	**Description**
Next Inspection Due:	**Time Since Overhaul**	**Mech. Cert. # or Repair Station #** ______

☐ **HUB & BLADE INSPECTIONS, REPAIRS AND ALTERATIONS**

Year: ________ **Date:**	**Total Time in Service**	**Description**
Next Inspection Due:	**Time Since Overhaul**	**Mech. Cert. # or Repair Station #** ________

Year: ________ **Date:**	**Total Time in Service**	**Description**
Next Inspection Due:	**Time Since Overhaul**	**Mech. Cert. # or Repair Station #** ________

Year: ________ **Date:**	**Total Time in Service**	**Description**
Next Inspection Due:	**Time Since Overhaul**	**Mech. Cert. # or Repair Station #** ________

HUB & BLADE INSPECTIONS, REPAIRS AND ALTERATIONS ☐

Year: ______ Date:	Total Time in Service	Description
Next Inspection Due:	Time Since Overhaul	Mech. Cert. # or Repair Station # ______

Year: ______ Date:	Total Time in Service	Description
Next Inspection Due:	Time Since Overhaul	Mech. Cert. # or Repair Station # ______

Year: ______ Date:	Total Time in Service	Description
Next Inspection Due:	Time Since Overhaul	Mech. Cert. # or Repair Station # ______

☐ AIRWORTHINESS DIRECTIVES

Year: ______ Date:	Total Hours	Complied by the following:
A.D. #		
Next Inspection Due: ______	Mech. Cert. # or Repair Station # ______	

Year: ______ Date:	Total Hours	Complied by the following:
A.D. #		
Next Inspection Due: ______	Mech. Cert. # or Repair Station # ______	

Year: ________ Date:	Total Hours	Complied by the following:
A.D. #		
Next Inspection Due: ________	Mech. Cert. # or Repair Station # ________	

Year: ________ Date:	Total Hours	Complied by the following:
A.D. #		
Next Inspection Due: ________	Mech. Cert. # or Repair Station # ________	

☐ AIRWORTHINESS DIRECTIVES

Year: ________

Date:

Total Hours

Complied by the following:

A.D. #

Next Inspection Due: ________

Mech. Cert. # or Repair Station # ________

Year: ________

Date:

Total Hours

Complied by the following:

A.D. #

Next Inspection Due: ________

Mech. Cert. # or Repair Station # ________

AIRWORTHINESS DIRECTIVES ☐

Year: ________ Date:	Total Hours	Complied by the following:
A.D. #		
Next Inspection Due: ________	Mech. Cert. # or Repair Station # ________	

Year: ________ Date:	Total Hours	Complied by the following:
A.D. #		
Next Inspection Due: ________	Mech. Cert. # or Repair Station # ________	

☐ FACTORY BULLETINS

Year: ______ Date:	Total Time in Service	Complied by the following:
Next Inspection Due:	Factory Bulletin #	

Mech. Cert. # or Repair Station # ______

Year: ______ Date:	Total Time in Service	Complied by the following:
Next Inspection Due:	Factory Bulletin #	

Mech. Cert. # or Repair Station # ______

Year: ______ Date:	Total Time in Service	Complied by the following:
Next Inspection Due:	Factory Bulletin #	

Mech. Cert. # or Repair Station # ______

Year: ______ Date:	Total Time in Service	Complied by the following:
Next Inspection Due:	Factory Bulletin #	

Mech. Cert. # or Repair Station # ______

☐ FACTORY BULLETINS

Year: ______ Date:	Total Time in Service	Complied by the following:
Next Inspection Due:	Factory Bulletin #	

Mech. Cert. # or Repair Station # ____________________

Year: ______ Date:	Total Time in Service	Complied by the following:
Next Inspection Due:	Factory Bulletin #	

Mech. Cert. # or Repair Station # ____________________

FACTORY BULLETINS ☐

Year: ______ Date:	Total Time in Service	Complied by the following:
Next Inspection Due:	Factory Bulletin #	

Mech. Cert. # or Repair Station # ______

Year: ______ Date:	Total Time in Service	Complied by the following:
Next Inspection Due:	Factory Bulletin #	

Mech. Cert. # or Repair Station # ______

Notes

Notes

Notes